No Lex 12-12

FAMOUS FIGURES OF

# GERONIMO

THE AMERICAN FRONTIER

## FAMOUS FIGURES OF THE AMERICAN FRONTIER

BILLY THE KID

BUFFALO BILL CODY

CRAZY HORSE

DAVY CROCKETT

GEORGE CUSTER

WYATT EARP

GERONIMO

JESSE JAMES

ANNIE OAKLEY

SITTING BULL

# FAMOUS FIGURES OF

# GERONIMO

## THE AMERICAN FRONTIER

## BILL AND DORCAS THOMPSON

CHELSEA HOUSE PUBLISHERS
PHILADELPHIA

Thanks to the Hartpence family for their many kindnesses and friendship, and for their introduction to Jim Gallagher, whose encouragement and advice helped us in writing this book. We are grateful for the many excellent sources that gave us an understanding of the Apache people as they struggled to survive in a changing world.

Produced for Chelsea House by
OTTN Publishing, Stockton, NJ


**CHELSEA HOUSE PUBLISHERS**
Editor in Chief: Sally Cheney
Associate Editor in Chief: Kim Shinners
Production Manager: Pamela Loos
Art Director: Sara Davis
Series Designer: Keith Trego

First Printing

1 3 5 7 9 8 6 4 2

The Chelsea House World Wide Web address is
http://www.chelseahouse.com

Library of Congress Cataloging-in-Publication Data

Thompson, William, 1931-
Geronimo / William and Dorcas Thompson.
    p.    cm. – (Famous figures of the American frontier)
Includes bibliographical references and index.
Summary: Examines the life of the Apache chief Geronimo, who led one of the last Indian uprisings.
    ISBN 0-7910-6491-3 (alk. paper)
    ISBN 0-7910-6492-1 (pbk.: alk. paper)
1. Geronimo, 1829-1909–Juvenile literature. 2. Apache Indians–Biography–Juvenile literature. 3. Apache Indians–Wars–Juvenile literature. [1. Geronimo, 1829-1909. 2. Apache Indians–Biography. 3. Indians of North America–New Mexico–Biography.] I. Title. II. Series.

E99.A6 G3275 2001
979.004'972–dc21
[B]                                                          2001028865

# CONTENTS

The Apache leader Geronimo strikes a defiant pose. For more than 20 years, Geronimo was involved in a struggle to protect his tribe's homeland in the Southwest from being taken by the U.S. government.

# Geronimo's Legacy

Early one bright spring morning, thousands of excited people began to fill the streets of Washington, D.C., eager to watch the greatest parade the city had yet seen. On this day, March 5, 1905, Theodore Roosevelt was being officially *inaugurated* as the 26th president of the United States.

For over three hours, 35,000 people passed in front

of the White House, where President Roosevelt stood watching. The parade included the governors of 15 states, cadets from West Point, and soldiers from the Seventh *Cavalry* of the U.S. Army, as well as marching bands from as far away as the Philippine Islands. As the crowds yelled and threw their hats into the air, six mounted Indian chiefs, each wearing tribal dress, came riding down Pennsylvania Avenue.

When Woodworth Clum, a member of the parade committee, recognized the legendary Apache leader Geronimo, he was puzzled. He turned and asked the president, "Why did you include the greatest single-handed murderer in American history?"

Roosevelt's answer was simple: "I wanted to give the people a good show."

Geronimo, the great warrior of the Apache Indians, had once been put into chains by Woodworth Clum's father, John Clum. Thirty years before, John Clum had been an Indian agent in Arizona. He had known the murdering Geronimo well—or at least he thought he did.

Others saw Geronimo in the same way as John and Woodworth Clum. At Geronimo's death in

February 1909, *Harper's Weekly*, a popular news-paper, had this to say:

> The death of Geronimo, the famous Apache chief, marks the passing of one of the most cruel and bloodthirsty Indians that ever terrorized the settlers on the Western plains. . . . He was typical of what a really "bad Indian" might be.

But an editorial in the *New York Times* from the same period offers a very different viewpoint:

> Now that all the obituaries of Geronimo have been printed, and everybody has been reminded of what a cruel and bloodthirsty wretch he was, it is only fair to recall the fact that while all the charges against him are true, they are so only from the white man's point of view. . . . The white settlers in the Southwest, were for Geronimo, invading aliens, ruthlessly taking a country to which they had no claim or title, and making life impossible for the Indians. . . . [They were] in short, enemies to be driven away if possible, and to be killed if necessary. That is exactly the way we or any other race would have proceeded to make war on the invaders.

Was Geronimo a mass murderer of innocent victims, as Mr. Clum believed? Or was Geronimo a warrior protecting his people?

The rugged, rocky landscape of Geronimo's childhood home in present-day Arizona. The Apaches were determined to hold onto their lands. They had fought for years with Spanish and Mexican troops, and gained a reputation for cunning and ferocity in battle.

# Growing up as
# an Apache

In the southwestern part of North America, around 1820 a baby boy named Goyahkla was born. His father, Taklishim, was the son of Mahko, chief of an Apache band. His mother had a Spanish name, Juana—possibly because she had been captured by the Spanish as a girl and had once been a slave.

Many subdivisions of the Apache tribe lived in that

area. Some were hostile to one another, while others were closely tied together by language, custom, and *intermarriage*. Five bands that were very close were the Bedonkohes, the Chiricahua, the Nednai, the Mimbrenos, and the Warm Springs. Goyahkla grew up among the Bedonkohes, who lived in the mountains near the Gila River in Arizona.

Since Apaches named their children by some personality trait or a certain circumstance, we can guess why Juana and Taklishim called their son Goyahkla, "One Who Yawns." One day, this name would be changed to Geronimo, a name that would be feared throughout the entire country.

His childhood, though, seems to have been happy and free. As an old man, he remembered the peacefulness of his early years: "As a babe I rolled on the dirt floor of my father's tipi, or hung in my *tsoch* [the Apache word for cradle] at my mother's back, or suspended from the bough of a tree. I was warmed by the sun, rocked by the winds, and sheltered by the trees as other Indian babies."

Like other Apache children, Goyahkla loved the land where he was born. He believed the Great Spirit had created the Apaches and their homeland for one another. All his life he believed that Apaches would become sick and die if they were separated from the land of their birth.

Apaches cherished their children, so Goyahkla grew up with plenty of attention from his parents. Taklishim told him about great deeds of war, how to make a bow and arrow, and how to hunt and care for horses. Juana taught him stories of the origin of the Apaches and how to pray to Usen, the Supreme Being, from whom everything came.

Goyahkla began more serious training when he was eight, when he learned to jump into an ice-covered creek before the sun came up, run up and down a mountain without drinking even a mouthful of water, and move quietly through the trees in preparation for a raid. As the final part of his training for manhood, Goyahkla was taken to a remote area and left alone with no food. He was expected to live off the land and find his way back home. Goyahkla succeeded well in all these lessons.

Goyahkla had lots of time to play between his lessons. He was a

The abilities the young Apache developed were intended to prepare him to be a strong warrior. While still a teenager, Goyahkla would be ready to be admitted to the council of warriors.

good swimmer by the time he was eight, and he joined other boys in war games. They competed against each other in footraces, tug-of-war, horse races, and wrestling matches–games any young boy might enjoy. He especially enjoyed practicing with the bow and arrow and became very good at using this weapon.

When Goyahkla was about 15, his father died after a long illness. Goyahkla watched as Taklishim was dressed in his best clothes. Then Taklishim's face was painted and he was wrapped in a rich blanket. Goyahkla followed as his father was carried to the mountains. Taklishim's horse walked behind his body, and the tribe wailed in a long procession down the mountain. According to tradition, the horse was killed, Taklishim's property given away, his body placed in a cave, and then the grave was sealed with stones.

Goyahkla could no longer be a boy. From that day on, he took care of his mother, as was the custom, for she never married again.

Sometime after his father's funeral, Goyahkla and his mother traveled south from their home to Mexico. His sister had married Juh, an Apache of the Nednai band, who lived in the rugged Sierra

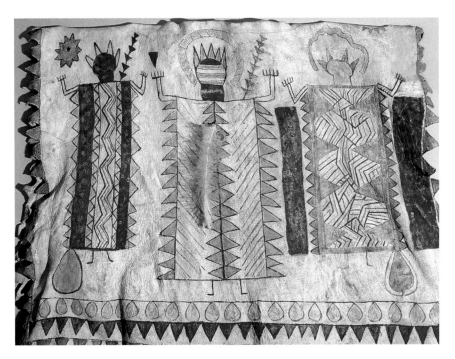

An Apache warrior's cloak. The figures on the cloak represent a god and spirits, which would protect the wearer.

Madre Mountains. The Nednais, the wildest of all the Apaches, were continually in conflict with the Mexicans.

The hostility between the Apaches and the Mexicans had existed for many years. During the 16th century, Spanish *conquistadors* became rulers of the native population in Mexico. The Spanish sent slave-catching expeditions to find workers for their mines, and the Spanish encouraged other Indian tribes to join them against the Apaches. As a result, the Apaches were driven into the mountains.

They responded with frequent raids against Mexico.

Mexico became independent from Spain in 1821, but the new government inherited the fight with the Apaches. Indian tribes would regularly bring terror to the countryside, raiding farms and towns, stealing cattle and killing people.

At one time the Mexican government paid a **bounty**, or reward, of 100 **pesos** for the scalp of an Apache man, 50 pesos for that of a woman, and 25 pesos for a child's scalp. (The peso is a Mexican unit of money.) Policies like this one only increased the hatred between the two sides.

When Goyahkla and his mother visited Juh, Goyahkla experienced his first taste of real battle. He was admitted into the council of warriors, and he began to put into practice the art of warfare he had learned as a young boy.

While with the Nednais, when he was 17 or 18, Goyahkla met a beautiful young woman named Alope. He paid her father many ponies, which he had stolen on raids, for permission to marry her. Soon after they were married, he left the Nednais and returned to his homeland with his wife and mother.

Not far from his mother's tepee, he made a new

home for him and his wife. He and Alope settled there among his people and had three children. Goyahkla loved his family and he wanted to give them the same happy childhood he had experienced. But future events would put an end to that hope.

# GOYAHKLA BECOMES GERONIMO

A group of Apaches ride into Mexico in this painting by Edward S. Curtis. During such a visit to Mexico, tragedy befell Goyahkla. As a result, he harbored a bitter hatred against Mexicans for the rest of his life.

After years of conflict, the Mexican state of Chihuahua decided to seek peace with the Apaches. The Mexicans encouraged the Apaches to trade with them. The Indians were pleased with the opportunity and began to make trips into the towns of Chihuahua.

One day a band of Apaches, including the young warrior Goyahkla, went into Mexico with their goods—

baskets, vegetables, hides, and supplies. They traveled with their families, under the leadership of Chief Mangas Coloradas. When they reached Mexico, they set up camp outside the city of Janos in Chihuahua. There they left the women and children, while the men went into town to trade. Older men stayed in the camp to act as guards.

The news spread to the neighboring state of Sonora that the Apaches were in Janos. Unlike the Chihuahuans, the Sonorans were tired of Indian raids and wanted revenge. They sent troops into Chihuahua to find the Apaches there.

Once the soldiers from Sonora found the Apache camp, they pretended to be friendly and brought *mescal* to the camp guards. When the guards were drunk and sleeping, the soldiers killed them and invaded the camp. They *massacred* and scalped many women and children, capturing others to take as slaves. At least 21 people were killed, and 62 women and children were seized for slavery. Only a few escaped.

When the men returned from trading in Janos, they were met by the few women and children who were left. After the survivors told their story, the men waited until dark and then cautiously approached their camp. Goyahkla found the bodies of his mother, wife, and three children, who had all been massacred by the Mexican troops. He silently turned away and stood for a long time by the river, lost in his grief.

That same night the tribe held a council and decided that since they had only 80 warriors and were deep inside Mexican territory, they would head home. Silently, they left their dead and returned to Arizona. As Goyahkla walked, he barely knew what he was doing. He had no feeling, no purpose, no desire even to eat. He said nothing and no one talked with him. No one else had lost as many family members as he had.

When they reached their home, Goyahkla looked for a last time at the things Alope had made and at the playthings of his three little ones. Then he burned his mother's tepee and all her property, as well as everything he owned. In doing so, he was following the Apache tradition when someone died.

Sometime later, Goyahkla went far into the mountains. Anger was deep within him and he longed for vengeance. Legends tell that as he grieved, alone in the high rocks, he heard a voice. Quietly, it spoke his name four times (four was a sacred number to the Apaches). He was told that no bullets would kill him and that his own arrows would be guided into the hearts of his enemies. Goyahkla always believed he had received the gift of the "Power" that night, a power that came on an Indian suddenly and could only be given by the Supreme Being. For the rest of his life, Goyahkla was credited with amazing abilities, such as protection in battle and being able to foresee events.

Goyahkla returned home, but he was never content there again. He vowed vengeance upon the Mexican troops who had murdered his family. Whenever anything reminded him of the happy life he had once enjoyed, hate would fill his heart until it ached for revenge. That hatred would drive his life and determine his future.

But he was not alone in his grief and hatred. The whole tribe felt deeply the loss of their people in the massacre at Janos. Mangas Coloradas called a council, and his warriors agreed to take the *warpath* against the Mexicans. They began to gather weapons and supplies for the battle ahead.

Goyahkla was chosen to get help from other Apache bands. First he went to Cochise, a great warrior and chief of the Chiricahua Apaches. Next he

A drawing of Cochise, the most famous Apache leader of the 1850s and 1860s. Cochise was the son-in-law of Mangas Coloradas, the leader of Goyahkla's Apache band.

went to Juh, his brother-in-law in Mexico. Both agreed to join Mangas Coloradas and his warriors.

The three tribes prepared for battle. They rode no horses, for they wanted to move with secrecy. With Goyahkla as their guide, they went far south into Mexico, traveling 14 hours a day, stopping only for meals. They covered about 45 miles every day. In order to keep their movements hidden, they followed rivers and mountain ranges in the desert land. Finally, they reached their destination, the Mexican town of Arispe. Here Goyahkla knew they would find the soldiers who had murdered their people. They posted sentinels that night and rested.

On the first day, they had a brief *skirmish* with the Mexicans. On the following day, at about 10 in the morning, a large force of Mexican soldiers rode out of the town. Two companies of cavalry and two of *infantry* faced the Apaches. Goyahkla asked the chiefs if he could lead the battle. Because he had suffered more deeply than the others, they gave him that honor.

Goyahkla was determined to prove himself worthy of their trust. He formed a semicircle with his warriors and led a charge against the Mexicans. As he fought, he was filled with fury as he thought again and again of his murdered family. When the two-hour battle was over, the Apache warriors had won

Tradition says that during the battle, the Mexicans cried out in fear when they saw Goyahkla's savage attack. They prayed to St. Jerome (right) to save them from this demon. The Indians didn't understand what the Mexicans were yelling, but they began to imitate the sound of the Mexicans' cries. "Geronimo! Geronimo!" they shouted. Thus was born a name that would go down in history.

complete victory. Over the bloody battlefield, covered with the bodies of Mexican soldiers, rang a loud war cry. Hot with victory, the Apache braves surrounded Goyahkla and made him the war chief of all the Apaches.

Goyahkla also received a new name. He would be called Geronimo for the rest of his life. It is this name that would strike fear in the hearts of many.

Among his own people, Geronimo's importance grew. As evidence of this, he took two more wives. (Only the more powerful warriors and leaders could afford to support more than one wife.) During the course of his long life, he had a total of eight or nine wives. They and their children would suffer with him through the years ahead.

His second wife, Chee-hash-kish, the mother of a son, was eventually captured by the Mexicans, and Geronimo never saw her again. His third wife and her child were killed when Mexican soldiers attacked his band while they were resting from a raid in Mexico. Their suffering fueled Geronimo's hatred of the Mexicans.

Before long, though, Geronimo would have another enemy as well. In fact, his difficulties were just beginning.

Geronimo surveys the landscape while leading a raiding party. He would soon face a new enemy in his battle to defend the Apache homeland—the growing United States.

# Conflict with the United States

As Geronimo and the Apaches were taking their revenge against the Mexicans, they had no idea that to the east, some 30 million people believed their *destiny* was to extend the borders of the United States from the Atlantic to the Pacific Ocean. Thousands of U.S. citizens were pouring into Indian territory, overwhelming the tribes who depended on the land for their lives.

Many of the people settling the West had come to Indian territory to make whatever profit they could from the land. They were ready to fight for a new life, and they had no love for the Indians, who seemed to stand in their way.

The United States government also saw Native Americans as an obstacle to the settlement of the western lands. Beginning in the 1820s, the government's solution was to put Indians on land set apart just for them, called *reservations*.

> The Apaches did not understand the idea of property ownership. In their minds all the land belonged to Usen, the Supreme Being.

Indian agents, working for the U.S. government, were sent to manage the welfare of the Indians. However, because of many dishonest and inefficient agents, the reservations were often poorly run, and many Indians were mistreated.

A few years before the massacre of Geronimo's family, war had broken out between Mexico and the United States. It lasted from 1846 until 1848, when the Treaty of Guadalupe Hidalgo was signed. That treaty gave the Southwest, the ancestral home of the Apaches, to the United States. In the treaty, the American government promised to protect Mexico

U.S. troops storm the Mexican stronghold at Monterey, California, in September 1846, during the Mexican-American War. The war enabled the United States to acquire a vast amount of land from Mexico: California and the New Mexico territory, which included the present-day states Nevada and Utah, as well as parts of Colorado, Wyoming, Arizona, and New Mexico— where Geronimo and the Apaches lived.

from Indian raids. The Americans also promised to return to the Mexicans any captives the Apaches had taken. This agreement quickly created tension between the United States and the Apaches.

In 1851 the U.S. government wanted to map the boundary with Mexico. The mappers set up a head-quarters in Arizona, where they were visited by Mangas Coloradas and his people, probably right after their raid at Arispe.

While the chief and his band were camped near the commission, two Mexican boys, held captive by the Apaches, escaped and fled to the American camp. The Americans refused to return them. The Apaches considered these captives members of their families and resented having them taken away.

This kind of misunderstanding happened often. The Indians' mistrust increased as trains and stage-coaches brought more easterners through the West. Gold and other minerals were found on Indian land, and as a result, miners and settlers moved in. They built towns on land that had been set aside for the Indians. Tension continued to grow.

When Mangas Coloradas attempted to talk with some miners about living together in peace, he was tied to a tree and severely beaten. At about the same time, Cochise was accused by an army officer of kidnapping a white boy. Even though Cochise denied the accusation and agreed to help find the boy, he was arrested. Cochise escaped, taking some hostages with him. Some of his relatives, still held by the American soldiers, were killed, and Cochise killed the hostages he had taken in response.

Around 1860, open warfare broke out between the Apaches and the Americans. Mangas Coloradas, Cochise, Geronimo, and Juh went on the warpath together. The Apaches attacked settlements and supply trains, killing many people and disrupting travel through the territory. The U.S. Army responded by sending more troops. The Apaches attacked an army force moving through Apache Pass, a vital route through the mountains. Because of the Americans' use of a *howitzer*, the Apaches had to retreat. However, they had inflicted heavy losses without losing many of their own warriors.

For a time, the Indian warriors hoped they were recapturing their land. Afraid of the Apaches, white settlers deserted some mines and towns. When the Civil War began in 1861, the authorities in Washington withdrew many troops to fight in the East. However, bloody conflicts continued throughout the 1860s. These recurring struggles became known as the Apache Wars. Geronimo acted as war chief, organizing attacks and directing battles.

In January 1863, a group of gold seekers traveling to California managed to capture Mangas Coloradas to

During the Apache Wars, Geronimo developed a lasting mistrust of American troops. In his eyes, the American officers never hesitated to wrong the Indians; they reported to their superiors only what the Indians did and not misdeeds by their own soldiers.

assure their safe journey through hostile Apache land. However, an army officer in the area took Mangas from the miners. That night he had Mangas shot. An army surgeon cut off Mangas's head, boiled it, and sent his skull to Washington, D.C., for study. Years later, Geronimo said that this treachery, against a man who had wanted peace, was perhaps the greatest wrong ever done to the Apaches.

After years of conflict with American forces, Cochise began to realize that his small band could not continue fighting. A peace conference was set up with General Oliver O. Howard, who had been sent by the U.S. government to settle Indians on reservations. They reached an agreement on October 13, 1872. Cochise and the Apache warriors, including Geronimo, would end the fighting. In return, the government would give them land on which to settle. The Apaches were given a reservation along the Arizona and New Mexico border.

Cochise kept his pledge to live quietly on the reservation. He died in 1874 without going on the warpath again. However, Geronimo continued to make raids into Mexico. He did not believe his agreement with the Americans had anything to do with his revenge against his old enemies. As a result

This cartoon, showing an Indian chasing General Oliver O. Howard around a large rock, appeared in a humor magazine in the 1870s. It poked fun at the army's lack of success in the Apache Wars with a fake message from the general: "I am still pursuing the Indians."

of these attacks, the people living in the Southwest continued to fear the Apaches.

In 1871, General George Crook was sent west to complete the task of settling Indians on reservations. In November of 1872, Crook began a campaign against the hostile tribes who continued to attack settlers. With the help of Native American scouts, Crook was able to capture most of the hostile Indians and bring order to the Southwest.

Although the U.S. government was pleased with this accomplishment, the outcome for Geronimo was not so positive.

# Geronimo Becomes a Renegade

Geronimo stands on the right in this photo, accompanied by several well-armed members of his tribe.

In August of 1874, Indian agent John Clum arrived at the San Carlos Reservation in Arizona. Clum was an honest and able 23-year-old who liked the Indians and was able to work with them. He treated them fairly and made sure they received their full rations. Clum helped to develop the best relations the Americans and Indians had known since the Apache Wars began.

However, in the same year the Bureau of Indian Affairs in Washington began its plan to place all Indians in Arizona and New Mexico on one reservation. The bureau's argument was that a single reservation would be easier to manage, but the real reason may have been that Americans wanted more land for themselves.

General Crook strongly opposed the decision to move all the Native Americans to one reservation. Crook realized it was dangerous to put different tribes, who often did not get along, together in one place. He also knew that the land at San Carlos was not good and that the area was too small to house so many Indians.

The San Carlos Reservation—a dusty, dry place with temperatures that reached as high as 110 degrees in the shade—was chosen as the place where Indians from other reservations would settle. Soon, more than 4,000 Indians were living at San Carlos.

One group forced to move were the Chiricahua. Cochise's son Taza, who was now chief, reluctantly agreed to move. He realized he had little choice because of the strength of the American army in the area. Geronimo, still living with the Chiricahuas, also agreed to be transferred with his family group. But then he and Juh, with about 40 of their relatives, fled to the mountains. Once again, Geronimo lived off the land and made frequent raids upon the white settlers. During June and July of 1875, they killed 20 people and stole about 200 head of livestock.

Agent Clum was deeply angered that Geronimo did not go to San Carlos. From that time on, Geronimo became Clum's enemy. Clum blamed Geronimo for every raid made by any Indian band. Geronimo's name became known throughout the country and he began to acquire a reputation as a vicious killer.

Geronimo did not see things in the same way as white men like John Clum. He felt he had the freedom to go where he wanted. In his eyes, Agent Clum had no authority over him.

After leaving the Chiricahuas, Geronimo, Juh, and their families went to the Warm Springs Reservation, just west of San Carlos. They lived among the peaceable Indians there, but they continued making frequent raids, mostly into Mexico.

In 1877, when he learned that Geronimo was at Warm Springs, Clum went there to arrest him. He took Indian police with him to remove Geronimo and his followers to San Carlos, where they would be tried for murder and robbery. Once in Warm

Springs, the police hid, while Clum asked Geronimo to meet him. Geronimo agreed—and in a surprise move, he was surrounded and captured. He was put into chains and sent to San Carlos.

As he approached San Carlos, Geronimo expected to die. That may have been John Clum's plan, but fortunately for Geronimo, Clum had a disagreement with his superiors and resigned his position as Indian agent. The new agent released Geronimo from his chains and allowed him to live freely on the San Carlos Reservation.

After Clum's resignation, however, conditions became worse at the reservation. Indians were sick with *malaria* and dying of *smallpox*. Others were hungry and poorly clothed. Corrupt agents stole their supplies and sold them to nearby townspeople. Many Indians became angry and bitter.

In April of 1878, Geronimo fled the reservation, along with Juh. At around the same time, another Apache warrior, Victorio, left with about 50 warriors loyal to him. Victorio's ruthless killings were far worse than anything the people of the Southwest had yet experienced. Since he left about the same time as Geronimo, many Americans assumed the two of them had combined their forces.

Geronimo grew tired of the constant hiding. In the fall of 1879, while Victorio was still slashing his way across the area, Geronimo told the Americans he wanted to surrender. He said he would not go on the warpath again. In early 1880, an agreement was reached, and Geronimo returned to San Carlos.

For several months, Geronimo lived among the other reservation Indians and tried to adjust to life at San Carlos. However, an Indian prophet, Noch-ay-del-klinne, began to stir up the Apaches by telling them he could restore their dead chiefs to life. He predicted that white people would one day be gone and the land would be theirs again. The prophet's fiery preaching inspired Geronimo.

The religious passion that Noch-ay-del-klinne brought to the Indians frightened the settlers, and in August of 1880, troops were sent to arrest the prophet. In the struggle, Noch-ay-del-klinne was

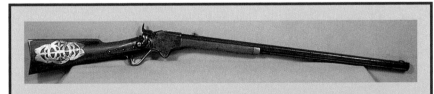

This .44-caliber Spencer carbine, which belonged to Geronimo, was one of the most popular rifle models used during the Civil War.

killed, along with 18 other Indians and eight soldiers. The Americans feared an Indian uprising, so
more troops were sent to San Carlos. Geronimo and
Juh were afraid they might be arrested. For the second time, they fled the reservation. They took with
them 74 warriors and their families.

On their flight to Mexico they killed everybody
they met, stealing horses and supplies. After finding
safety in the Sierra Madre Mountains at Juh's
stronghold, they were joined by other bands that
had left San Carlos.

For over a year, Geronimo and Juh led their warriors on successful raids against Mexican towns.
They also surprised the Indians at San Carlos by
returning in April 1882 and *coercing* some of the
people to go with him. Eventually, though,
Geronimo needed to make a raid into Arizona to

To find Geronimo, General
Crook hired Apaches from
the reservations to serve
as his scouts. These men
were willing to hunt their
fellow Apaches because
they felt the outlaw band
had brought much trouble
upon their people.

pick up ammunition for his American-built guns. That raid was to prove his undoing. While in Arizona, a warrior named Tsoe, one of those Indians forced to leave San Carlos, deserted Geronimo. He went back to his family, who were still living on the Arizona reservation.

When Tsoe returned, he met General Crook at San Carlos. He told him of the time he had spent with Geronimo in the Sierra Madre Mountains. Tsoe agreed to guide General Crook to Geronimo's camp. The American force reached Juh's stronghold in May of 1883. Geronimo and most of the warriors were out hunting, so Crook's forces easily captured the Apache camp.

The Apaches eventually agreed to talk with General Crook. After lengthy discussions, they reached a peace agreement. Geronimo and the others returned once again to live at San Carlos. Only Juh, with a few of his followers, refused and continued to remain hostile.

For the first time, peace seemed likely in the Southwest. But Geronimo would break out of the reservation one more time. This time, his action would spell disaster for the Apache people and separate them from the land they loved.

# SURRENDER

Geronimo and the remains of his Apache band are escorted to Fort Bowie, Arizona, by troops under the command of General Nelson Miles. The Apache Wars ended with Geronimo's surrender in September 1886.

The Indians lived peacefully at San Carlos for over a year. However, changes in the government officers who ran the reservation made the Apaches uneasy. Also, Geronimo knew that newspapers were asking for his death. On May 17, 1885, Geronimo left the reservation again, this time with 35 men and 109 women and children. Other leaders fled with him.

The Apaches, feeling they had nothing to lose, helped themselves to horses and supplies as they fled to Mexico, killing whoever was in their way. By June 10, Geronimo had crossed the border and rejoined Juh. From their hideout in the Sierra Madre Mountains, the Apaches made raids on Mexican towns and into the United States. The population of the area was constantly in an uproar, demanding the final destruction of the Apaches. General Crook decided to invade the warriors' camp again.

In November, Crook sent troops into Mexico. With the help of friendly Indian scouts, his men were able to find Juh's new mountain stronghold. Geronimo sent word to the Americans that he would talk with them. Both sides, heavily armed, met in a conference. Geronimo spoke again of his fears while at San Carlos and insisted that he talk personally with General Crook.

On March 25, 1886, a conference was held between Crook and the Apaches. Geronimo explained their reasons for leaving the reservation and said they only wanted to live at peace. General Crook replied that if Geronimo did not surrender unconditionally, U.S. troops would keep after him and kill him, even if it took 50 years.

Geronimo (seated, fourth from left) meets General George Crook (second from right) at Canyon de los Embudos in March 1886 for a three-day conference. Crook tried to persuade the Apache leader to surrender and return to the reservation. Although Geronimo initially accepted, he soon began raiding again.

An agreement was eventually made. Crook said the Indians must spend two years confined in the East with any family members who wanted to go with them. Geronimo agreed: "Once I moved about like the wind. Now I surrender to you and that is all. My heart is yours and I hope yours will be mine."

General Crook left for Arizona with some of the Indian band, convinced he had been successful. The others, including Geronimo, were to follow the next day. That night, though, a man named

Tribolett convinced Geronimo that he would be killed the minute he entered the United States. In the middle of the night, Geronimo fled with 20 warriors and some women and children.

Meanwhile, General Crook had informed Washington of the peace agreement. The U.S. government rejected the terms, because it wanted Geronimo tried—and hopefully hanged. When the news came a few days later that Geronimo had escaped, Crook was severely criticized. He asked to be relieved of his position, and General Nelson Miles was sent to take his place.

General Miles dismissed the Indian scouts and relied instead on a force of 5,000 soldiers, 25 percent of the entire U.S. Army at that time. They began a difficult and exhausting search for Geronimo. After months of searching, General Miles was not even able to sight Geronimo, much less enter into battle with the Apaches. Meanwhile, Geronimo continued to raid both the United States and Mexico. He even appeared at times near the San Carlos Reservation.

Miles finally spoke to some of Geronimo's relatives who were still on the reservation. Through them, he learned how he could contact Geronimo.

Eventually, he made contact with the Apache war chief and set up a conference. The place where they would meet was called Skeleton Canyon, just inside the U.S. border.

On September 4, General Miles arrived and held what would be the final conference with Geronimo. Geronimo was reluctant to surrender, but when other warriors decided to give up fighting, he felt he had no choice. When the Apaches learned that their families had already been shipped to Florida, they wanted to go there to be with them.

Geronimo and the others traveled with Miles and his soldiers to Fort Bowie in Arizona. Once there, Miles promised Geronimo that he would be with his family; in two years he would be allowed to live on a separate reservation where no one would harm him. He convinced Geronimo that the past was forgotten and that he would begin a new life once his prison time was over. After nearly 35 years, the Apache Wars were over at last.

Geronimo and his remaining people were boarded on trains to Florida. General Miles wanted to send Geronimo out of the area as quickly as possible in order to protect him from the whites living in the Southwest, who hated him.

However, army commander Philip Sheridan insisted that Geronimo stand trial in that part of the country. The Apache warriors were taken off the train at San Antonio, Texas, and held there, while their families were sent on to Florida. The warriors protested, but their pleas were ignored.

When General Sheridan learned that the warriors had been promised they would be sent to prison in Florida, he eventually shipped them out—but not to the fort where their families waited. Instead, he sent them to Fort Perkins. This fort was located outside Pensacola, Florida, 300 miles across the state from the Apache families at Fort Marion. Geronimo would not see his family for over a year.

During October of 1886, the U.S. Bureau of Indian Affairs decided that the children at Fort Marion should be sent to school. The bureau chose the Indian School at Carlisle, Pennsylvania. The Apaches resisted having their children separated from them, and even tried to hide them. As prisoners of war, however, there was little they could do.

The parents would have fought harder if they had known what would happen to many of their children. Some would die at Carlisle, or be sent home to die, as was the case with Chappo,

Apache prisoners, including Geronimo (front row, third from right), at a stop on the Southern Pacific Railroad. The prisoners were on their way to Florida when the train was stopped at San Antonio, Texas.

Geronimo's son. Of the 112 children sent to Carlisle over the next year, 27 died from disease. The health of the prisoners at Fort Marion was not much better.

However, conditions were far better at the Pensacola fort. The former warriors were put to work five days a week cleaning up the once abandoned fort. They worked hard in the fresh air and had plenty of food. Their health remained good. Colonel Langdon, the commander of the fort, came to understand the Indians and their longing for their families. As a result, he wrote his superiors and urged them to reunite the Apaches.

While at the fort, the 17 warriors became celebrities. The people of Florida did not hate the Apaches as did the people of the Southwest who had warred with them. Americans began flocking to see Geronimo and the other captives. The newspapers in Pensacola even advertised the prisoners as a tourist attraction. Geronimo and the others learned to profit from this popularity. They sold items they had made and even articles of their own clothing.

Because of the publicity the Indians received, the public became increasingly interested in their welfare. When Fort Marion was inspected, it was declared unfit for the prisoners there. On April 27, 1887, Geronimo and the other men at Fort Perkins were finally reunited with their families.

But Geronimo and the others still longed for their home in Arizona. They got an interpreter who lived with them to write a letter to General Stanley, who had helped them while they were in San Antonio. They wanted to know how long they would be in prison and when they would get the good land promised to them by General Miles. They never received an answer.

The next year, on May 13, 1888, nearly two years after his surrender, Geronimo and the others were sent to Mobile, Alabama, where the Apache band settled down on a military reservation of 2,000 acres, with sandy ridges and low-lying swamps. Each family had a log cabin of two rooms. Though the climate was still humid, the conditions were far better than at Fort Marion.

Their health problems continued, though. An investigation made in December 1889 discovered that in the three and a half years since the first Indians were sent east, there had been 89 deaths in the camps and 30 at Carlisle. One-fourth of the total Apache prison population had died.

But the Apaches tried to make the most of their time in Alabama. They built a village and managed to plant gardens in the sandy soil. Tourists began to arrive to see them just as they had in Florida. The Indians sold what they made and used that income to buy things for themselves. Geronimo learned to write his name in English, and he sold the bows and arrows he made.

The Apaches' time in this humid land was almost over, though. Soon, they would go to a new home.

This painting of Geronimo as an old man was made by Elbridge Burbank in 1898, when he visited the infamous chief at Fort Sill, Oklahoma. After settling down in Oklahoma, Geronimo became more a figure to be pitied than feared, making appearances at fairs and festivals, where he sold photographs of himself, buttons from his coats, and other souvenirs.

# A New Home in the West

The War Department considered different places to relocate the Apaches, such as Ohio and Illinois and even New England. The department did not want to send the prisoners to Arizona or New Mexico, because of the hatred the people there still had for the Apaches.

Comanche Indians, living near Fort Sill in the Oklahoma Territory, heard of the government's attempt to move the Apaches. The Comanches sympathized, and sent word to the U.S. authorities that they would agree to have the Indians live on their reservation.

Two army officers were sent to talk with the Apaches. Geronimo acted as their spokesperson. He and all the Indians were in complete agreement that they leave Alabama and settle in the Oklahoma Territory. Geronimo said: "I want to go away somewhere where we can farm, have cattle, cool water. . . . Young men, old men, women and children, all want to get away from here. . . . It is too hot and wet . . . too many of us die here."

On October 4, 1894, they were sent to Fort Sill. There were now only 296 Apaches, with 45 of their young people still at Carlisle. Hundreds of Comanches came to meet them. Since neither could speak the other's language, they had to talk in English through boys who had gone to Carlisle.

The Apaches first settled in huts along a creek, where they gathered beans from *mesquite* trees, a favorite food they had not tasted in years. The government provided cattle, and they began to learn ranching. After the first winter, they built homes in small villages scattered throughout the reservation.

In Oklahoma, the fierce Apache leader settled into farming life. Geronimo is shown here with his family on their melon farm.

Geronimo was one of the many who became farmers, and he was recognized as one of the best. Together, those who farmed raised more than 250,000 melons the first year. They also grew hay and corn.

Despite the changes in his life, Geronimo continued to be seen by many as a savage Indian. People were eager to see him, though, for he had become a celebrity. One of Geronimo's first interviews was with an artist, Elbridge Burbank, who had been sent to paint the portrait of the famous chief. The artist expected to see a vicious, bloodthirsty

> Many untrue stories were printed about Geronimo, and these increased his notoriety. One said that he had a blanket made of 100 white scalps taken during his last escape. Apaches, however, did not take scalps except on rare occasions, and Geronimo did not collect them.

savage locked up in a prison. He was surprised to find a kind old man, living in his own home, doing the housework for his sick wife. He watched as Geronimo swept the house and tenderly cared for his daughter.

Geronimo had not been at Fort Sill very long before he began to receive offers to appear at various events. Promoters knew of his fame and realized that Geronimo could attract a large crowd. He agreed; he knew these appearances would provide him with money, and they would also give him opportunities to ask for a return to his homeland. The government gave him permission to attend such events, and Geronimo began his travels.

On the way to these events, whenever the train would stop at a station, he would cut buttons from his coat and sell them for 25 cents. On the way to the next station, he would sew buttons back onto his coat from a supply he had brought with him, so that he could sell them again at the next stop. He also sold pictures of himself. Soon, he became a popular attraction at celebrations in Oklahoma. Sometimes he danced in front of the large crowds. Other times, he simply rode in a parade, wearing an Apache headdress with a streamer of eagles' feathers.

General Miles came to an exposition, and the two met one another for the first time in 12 years. At first Geronimo could hardly speak. Then, through an interpreter, his words poured out. First, he accused Miles of lying to him, making promises that had never been fulfilled. Then he asked Miles to help him return to Arizona. Miles refused, saying that the people of Arizona could now sleep in peace without fearing they would be killed.

In March of 1905, Geronimo traveled to Washington, D.C., for President Roosevelt's inauguration parade. Four days after the parade, Geronimo, along with five other Indian chiefs, met privately with the new president. Geronimo asked Roosevelt to let him return to Arizona. Once again, he was rebuffed. Roosevelt told him that because of the hatred against Geronimo in the West, he would not be able to live in peace in Arizona.

Geronimo continued to travel, but he was beginning to age. He was also becoming more absent-minded, and he had to reduce his public appearances. In February of 1909, back in Oklahoma, he decided to ride into the town of Lawton. He asked a white friend to get him whiskey, which was illegal for Indians to buy. Geronimo became intoxicated and, while riding home, fell off his horse. He lay in the cold through the night and wasn't discovered until the next morning.

> The word Geronimo is commonly used in the heat of battle. When soldiers parachuted from their planes in World War II, they would cry "Geronimo!" to signify their bravery.

After three days, he was taken to the hospital at Fort Sill. As he grew sicker, he rambled on about the massacre of his family and his lifelong hatred of the Mexicans. He died early in the morning of February 17, 1909. Geronimo was buried in the cemetery at Fort Sill.

Whatever else might be said of him—and many during his day called him a vicious, cold-blooded killer—Geronimo was an extremely determined, courageous warrior. He refused to give up the battle for his people and their land, regardless of the threat to his own life. Hero or villain, Geronimo remains one of the most fascinating figures of the American frontier.

1823 Goyahkla (later named Geronimo) is believed to have been born

1841 Goyahkla visits Juh's stronghold in Mexico with his mother, Juana; accepted in Council of Warriors; marries Alope

1848 The Treaty of Guadalupe Hidalgo, ending the Mexican-American War, is signed, giving control of the Apache homeland to the U.S. government

1850 Mangas Coloradas takes band to Janos, Mexico, to trade; Goyahkla's family and mother travel with them; Goyahkla's family is massacred by Mexican soldiers from Sonora; Indian bands under Mangas Coloradas, Juh, and Cochise unite for battle; Goyahkla takes leadership of the battle and is renamed "Geronimo"

1851 Geronimo takes two more wives and has three children

1860 Apache Wars against Americans begin under leadership of Cochise and Mangas Coloradas; Geronimo begins battling with U.S. troops

1863 Mangas Coloradas is captured, shot, and beheaded

1871 General George Crook arrives to take command of military in the West

1872 Cochise surrenders and lives with his Chiricahua people on own reservation

1874 John Clum arrives at San Carlos Reservation as Indian agent; Cochise dies; Chiricahua Apaches moved to San Carlos Reservation

# CHRONOLOGY

**1875**    Geronimo agrees to go to San Carlos Reservation but flees instead

**1877**    John Clum arrests Geronimo at Warm Springs and takes him in chains to San Carlos; John Clum resigns and Geronimo is allowed freedom on reservation

**1878**    Geronimo leaves reservation with Juh; Victorio leaves separately and begins attacking settlers in the area

**1880**    Early in the year, Geronimo returns to San Carlos; in August, Geronimo again flees reservation and goes to Mexico with Juh

**1883**    Geronimo surrenders to General Crook; arrives back at San Carlos in February of 1884

**1885**    Geronimo again leaves San Carlos and returns to Mexico

**1886**    Geronimo surrenders to General Crook in March, but then flees into the mountains; General Crook resigns; General Nelson A. Miles sent to take his place; Geronimo surrenders to Miles in September; Geronimo and 16 Apache warriors are sent to Fort Perkins while their families are sent to Fort Marion

**1887**    Geronimo and the warriors at Fort Perkins are reunited with their families

**1888**    Geronimo and his family sent to Mobile, Alabama

**1894**    Remaining Apaches moved to Fort Sill, Oklahoma

**1905**    Geronimo rides in President Roosevelt's parade

**1909**    Geronimo dies on February 17

**bounty**–a reward for the capture of an outlaw.

**cavalry**–an army troop mounted on horses.

**coerce**–to force a person or people to do something.

**conquistadors**–Spanish fighting men who conquered Mexico and areas of South America in the 16th century.

**destiny**–fate; an unavoidable course of events.

**howitzer**–a short cannon used to fire projectiles.

**inaugurate**–to induct into a high office with ceremony.

**infantry**–foot soldiers.

**intermarriage**–marriage between members of different groups.

**malaria**–a disease caused by parasites in the red blood cells, transmitted by mosquitoes.

**massacred**–slaughtered; killed brutally.

**mescal**–a Mexican alcoholic beverage.

**mesquite**–spiny shrubs that grow in the Southwest and produce sweet pods.

**peso**–a Mexican unit of money, worth about a dollar in the 19th century.

**reservation**–a piece of public land set aside where Native Americans were forced live.

**skirmish**–a minor fight.

**smallpox**–an often fatal disease that causes pus-filled sores.

**warpath**–the route taken by Native Americans going on a warlike expedition; a hostile state of mind.

# FURTHER READING

Barrett, S.M. ed. *Geronimo: His Own Story as told to S.M. Barrett.* New York: Penguin Books, 1996.

Betezinez, Jason. *I Fought with Geronimo.* Lincoln: University of Nebraska Press, 1987.

Davis, Britton. *The Truth About Geronimo.* Lincoln: University of Nebraska Press, 1989.

Debo, Angie. *Geronimo: The Man, His Time, His Place.* Norman: University of Oklahoma Press, 1989.

Faulk, Odike. *The Geronimo Campaign.* New York: Oxford University Press, 1969.

Hermann, Spring. *Geronimo: Apache Freedom Fighter.* Springfield, N.J.; Enslow Publishers, 1997.

Melody, Michael E. *The Apache.* Philadelphia: Chelsea House Publishers, 1989.

Opler, Morris Edward. *An Apache Life Way: The Economic, Social and Religious Institutions of the Chiricauhua Indian.* Lincoln: University of Nebraska Press, 1987.

Schwarz, Melissa. *Geronimo: Apache Warrior.* Philadelphia: Chelsea House Publishers, 1991.

Shorto, Russell. *Geronimo and the Apache Struggle for Freedom.* Englewood Cliffs, N.J.: Silver Burdett Press, 1989.

# Picture Credits

**BILL THOMPSON** graduated from Boston University with a degree in education. After teaching history in public schools, Mr. Thompson earned a Master of Divinity from Colgate-Rochester and became a Presbyterian minister. He pastored in New York, New Jersey, and Florida. He and his wife, Dorcas, now live in Swarthmore, Pennsylvania.

**DORCAS (BOARDMAN) THOMPSON** graduated from Wheaton College in Illinois with a bachelor's degree in history. She taught history and social studies in Massachusetts, New York, and Pennsylvania. She has served as head librarian in a private school and worked as an editor for an educational publisher in Massachusetts. The Thompsons have one daughter, Rebecca Mandia, who is an elementary school teacher in Newtown, Pennsylvania.